Map of the
SELF

Poems by
Mona Dash

2025
Linen Press

Published by Linen Press, London 2025

8 Maltings Lodge
Corney Reach Way
London
W4 2TT

www.linen-press.com

© Mona Dash 2025

The right of Mona Dash to be identified as the author of this work has been asserted by her in accordance with the Copyright, Designs and Patents Act 1988. All rights reserved. This book is sold subject to the condition that it shall not, by way of trade or otherwise, be lent, resold, hired out, or otherwise circulated without the publisher's prior consent in any form of binding or cover other than that in which it is published and without a similar condition, including this condition, being imposed on the subsequent purchaser.

All names, characters, and incidents portrayed in this book are fictitious. No identification with actual persons (living or deceased) or places is intended nor should be inferred.

A CIP catalogue record for this book is available from the British Library.

Cover art and design: Lynn Michell

Typesetting by Blot Publishing: blot.co.uk

Printed and bound by Lightning Source ISBN 978-1-0683417-8-6

About the Author

Mona Dash is an award-winning author based in London. Her work includes her memoir A *Roll of the Dice,* a short story collection *Let Us Look Elsewhere*, a novel *Untamed Heart* and two collections of poetry, *A Certain Way* and *Dawn Drops*. Her work has been presented on BBC Radio 4, included in Best British Short Stories, and published in more than thirty-five anthologies. She is represented by Portobello Literary. She also works as a business leader in AI for a global tech company.

More details at www.monadash.net or follow on Instagram at monadash_

Books by Mona Dash

Dawn drops
(Writers Workshop, India, 2001)

Untamed Heart
(Tara India Research Press, 2016)

A Certain Way
(Skylark Publications, UK, 2017)

Roll of the Dice: a story of loss, love and genetics
(Linen Press, UK, 2019)

Let Us Look Elsewhere
(Dahlia Books, UK, 2021)

Praise and awards for Mona Dash's writing

Map of the Self

As (in)formally surprising, observant, contemporary – and full of care – as her short stories, Dash's poems do their thinking out loud, making unexpected and intimate connections that linger in the mind.
—Tony White, author

Mona Dash's poetry stresses an urge to become, and not just be. Her voice is that of the individual who comes with a history and a past, yet wills a transformation by the new experiences in journeys, settling elsewhere and building a home far away from the homeland. These are protest poems – bold, unapologetic and distinctive. – in a voice that will resonate with you long after you have read them.
—Bashabi Fraser, poet

Mona Dash's poetry listens deeply to absence and loss, to belonging and migration, crafting from them a resonant inner music that unsettles the terrain across geographies, histories, and even the personal body – a voice at once intimate and expansive, speaking through turmeric-stained memories, prowling silences, and the engulfing ambiguities of politics.
—Yogesh Patel, MBE

Mona Dash's Map of the Self is an engaging exploration of her world. In the process of defining herself, we are offered a glimpse of the challenges involved in determining her place in a complex and evolving universe. Her poetry grapples with the limits of being oneself, how the 'I' is so many things – a woman, an immigrant, a working mother, a poet, a lover – living with loss and disappointment, negotiating her way as she stretches the limits that shape her reality. She does this with flair and honesty.
—Shanta Acharya, poet

Mona Dash's Map of the Self, as the title alludes to, is predominantly about narratives about her own life, her "self", "map"ping her mind and body.

Whether it is the scorching incendiary process in 'The Making of a Goddess', or in 'The City, The Body' where she might "find something we don't know / we had never touched before, and we are transported. Another city, / like a body, full of possibility." Dash writes with an openness of heart and a sense of vulnerability that allows the reader to access her self's inner terrain.
—**Sudeep Sen, Poet**

Mona Dash has an enviable gift as a poet: taking the grandest of subjects, like migration or grief, and making them tangibly, viscerally real. The poems in 'Map of the Self' do this time and again, in language that's rich, sinuous and haunting. In her words, the biggest moments of life, remembering people loved and lost, and the grief that follows, are held lightly and tenderly. She reminds us that, even in the debris of any ending, healing is possible, and optimism remains.
— **Rishi Dastidar, poet**

Let Us Look Elsewhere

Shortlist SI Leeds Literary Award 2018, Shortlist Eyelands Book Award (Fiction) 2021, Shortlist Eastern Eye Award for Literature 2022
Shortlist Tagore Literary Prize 2023

A powerful collection of short stories.
—**Susheila Nasta**, SI Leeds Literary Prize chair of judges

These atmospheric stories travel across continents and time, offering surprising and intriguing incursions into the disparate moments of solitary lives.
—**Amanthi Harris**, Author

Mona Dash's short story collection is a fascinating concoction of characters and stories drawn from different corners of the world.
—**Asha Krishna** as reviewed in TSS Publishing

A wonderful, richly rendered and triumphant collection. Highly recommended.'
—**Irenosen Okojie**, Author

The stories are neatly laid out – beautifully crafted gems adorn this crown of a collection. A fascinating, bold debut that enthralls the reader right from the outset.' Read more at onerightword.blotspot.com

'Let Us Look Elsewhere by Mona Dash is a collection of short stories that will make you look elsewhere with eager eyes. I never knew where the author would take me next, to different times and places all across the world where I could learn about so many different lives and settings. Imaginative, risk-taking and always surprising, this collection of short stories is a joy to read.'
—Tracy Fells. Read more at The Literary Pig

A Roll of the Dice

Shortlist/ Finalist Eastern Eye Awards for Literature 2020
Finalist People's Book Prize 2020 (Non-Fiction)
Winner Eyelands Book Award 2020 (Memoir)

This is a story of loss, love and genetics... a very sensitive memoir about the adventure of a mother whose newborn baby's life is in danger. But this is just the beginning of an astonishing narrative of a contemporary life drama. Perfectly written in an unadorned, powerfully subtle style, demonstrating a deep knowledge of human – and especially female – nature. A Roll of the Dice is at the same time touching and riveting from cover to cover.
—Judges, Eyelands Book Awards 2020

Real, full of heartache, suffering and frustration of search for help and cure. Mona Dash takes us on a journey that I could only imagine. Beautifully written, honestly written. I am a writer of fiction. This is the real thing.
—**Stewart Foster**, author, Bubble Boy

A suspenseful novel which made me invest deeply in my protagonist and keep going till the nail-biting finish as to will they be okay. Mona also has a wonderful writing style. Sometimes stories can be great but the form prosaic. Mona's prose itself is delicious to read; her way of stringing words and sentences together. I recommend this book highly.
—**Shonali Bose**, filmmaker, writer

The language of this story is for the most part lyrical and even poetic, making it a highly engaging narrative, even as it also includes more technical passages describing medical conditions and procedures. This memoir is not a self-help book, but it is in the best sense inspirational.
—**From the review by America Hart** in the *Joao-Roque Literary Journal*

Mona Dash explains the consequences of passing on faulty genes to her two sons – and why she has relied continually on her faith and recital of the Hindu Maha Mrutyunjaya mantra.
—**Amit Roy**, Editor, Eastern Eye, UK

A Certain Way
Poet of Excellence award, Word Masala Foundation

Love is a crucial theme as important as her focus on the diasporic situation. Many kinds of love are celebrated in her poems – the love between man and woman, a mother's love, love for a father, love for a vampire, cynical love, wistful love, sensuous love, spiritual love and love that is lost. I applaud Mona Dash for essaying it with courage and flair. The author's true forte lies in her intimate poems of connectivity, about personal relationships with people, places and traditions.
—From the review by Debjani Chatterjee, MBE, poet, scholar in
The Book Review

Mona Dash's new collection of poems, A Certain Way, *displays a heightened sensibility that straddles the East and the West. The poems reflect the narrative of displacement and question tradition and modernity in language that is lyrical and full of strong imagery. This collection marks the arrival of a poet with an astute and sensitive awareness of what it means to arrive and leave.*
—From the review by Reshma Ruia, author in Episteme

There is a great calmness at the heart of tears in Mona Dash's windswept canvas of A Certain Way. A great objectivity and dispassionate detachment marks her profound involvement in the human experience of her own, yet universal suffering in the light, taut poems of time past, present, and yet to come – in which she locates the vast continents and depths of her mind, soul and body – uniting the acts of love, grief, and poetic release.
—From the review by Chandan Das (late), poet, English professor
in Muse India

*For my mother Mamata Dash, poet eternal, first reader,
and for being the reason writing has always been the normal thing to do.*

Contents

PART I: This, in our blood

Implications 3
The poet in business 4
Not knowing, Migration 5
Migrant Dilemma..........................7
Turmeric 8
Unbound feet............................. 9
The Making of a Goddess..................10
The subaltern cannot speak................12
For Plath, for Love........................13
Shakti 14
Christmas day walk 15
Unsaid, Unwritten........................16
The Waiting 17
Fool 18
Things in the fridge 19
Finding a Prayer.......................... 20
A world like this..........................21
The city, a body 22
Growing old 23
Infinity 24
Death, unknown 25
The body is no more......................26
This, in our blood 28

PART 2: The Runaway Poem

Crab self-defence.........................30
Drown...................................31
My Swan.................................32
The Sunrise.............................33
A dream in parts 34
A song in adversity 35
So you want to be a poet? 36
Untamed River...........................37
The Reluctant Love......................38
Trilogy of the Inevitable 41
You, soulmate...........................45
Touched 46
Moon by night 47
Love stories are sweet..................48
Be that man.............................49
The Runaway Poem 51

Acknowledgements 54

Part I
This, in our blood

Implications

Born and raised an Indian; not living in India
                      implied: *not Indian*
now British, not born in Britain
                      implied: *not British*
a mother, working full-time
                      implied: *not a mother*
a sales manager, a mother
                      implied: *not a sales manager*
a woman, a mother
                      implied: *not a woman*
an engineer, a poet
                      implied: *not an engineer*
In becoming more than I was meant to
                      implied: *a sense of erosion*
Venn-diagram like I seek
                      implied: *commonalities*
finding intersectionality
                      implied: *a pinpoint*

The poet in business

The poem in me
As if a silk scarf
Over a winter coat
    Unnecessary
    Fragile
    Bound to slip away
While I stand, crisp shirt
Tucked away neatly
Hair razor-sharp edged
Not one fly-away
Sky-high stilettos
    Unsteady
    Impractical
    Powerful
Painted long nails
A circle of a gold
chain, neat studs
As my voice drills numbers
Long excel sheets
Numbers, revenues, quarter
    On quarter
    Success
    Stock market
Perfect the role
Perfect the actor
Perfect the businesswoman

And the poem
Learns to stay a whisper
Just in passing
Just a flash of rainbow
Gone too soon
But not forgotten

Not knowing, Migration

The Banyan tree and the Oak
know the same language

Migration
is not an answer
nor a question
but a movement:
birds leave and return

Passport engraved with a stamp
coloured, dated. I
booked a ticket, landed in a country
closer to the poles from a country
closer to the equator

I didn't know
I would collect theories and words
presumptions and assumptions
on my back
like a feathery creature
feathers firm on the body
plucking one out
draws blood

Wonder why, how, I became
so many things at once
Emigrant, Immigrant, Migrant, Subaltern
concepts to luxuriate, nest in
I didn't know
that I could be invisible
when I enter a room

I didn't know
the philosophers, post-colonists

have labelled behaviour
branded my very soul
Hybridity, Provincialism, Orientalism
my shadows, my silhouettes defined
before I knew

Two-headed Janus
looking out, looking in
from where we came
to where we came

I thought I defined my self
I thought I was just I

Migrant Dilemma

Which country will I worry for
Which country should I cry for
The one I left, always home
The one I came to, forever home
If turmoil happens on every shore
Which one should I think about more?
Mourning in the morning
Or night time worrying
All over the world
A single narrative winning

And where did you all go
You poets and painters and singers
You asked us to *imagine*
and you left us asunder

Turmeric

On shop shelves, flavours of peach and turmeric
in little Kefir shots
Cranberry seeds and turmeric, masques in recyclable pots

Turmeric tastes on the tongue, lingering in infinite swirls
like jazz, renaissance, the beat. A turmeric rage grows
in homes, health shops, the patents, the recipes, lotions
on skin, turmeric in all its fine avatars

Somewhere, they love yellow milk, drink an aphrodisiac in a tall glass
team fish soft in thin gravy, liquid gold on shining white rice
and brides apply a creamy yellow paste wanting to look fair

But I remember
my mother's fingers, her tiny nails bitten to the quick,
mixing fish heads, pumpkin flowers
turmeric stains on the nail bed and folds

Yellow stains left on handles and plates and clothes
like on this scarf; her fingertips, golden dots,
                    from far-away home.

Unbound feet

First they bound our feet
bones broken into bite sized bits
chicken-wing dust post-dinner
flesh putrefied, perfumed
placed in lavish silk shoes
so small so beautiful
butterfly feet
that cannot stand firm
that cannot run
battered warped
lily-feet

then they didn't bind our feet
they just made sure when we ran
we were laughed at
when we tried to stand firm
the ground was pulled away
craters and venom beneath
then boulders tied to feet
we were pushed into the soil
living burial
even as we stand

soon they didn't have to try hard
the cages they grew us in
the boxes they stifled us in
broke our bodies and our breath
So they didn't have to

The Making of a Goddess

Resplendent Goddess
when you become
we will worship you
with flowers, the best
roses, we shall decree
lotuses, pink-gold, fifty-five petals no less
incense mesmerising intoxicating
only the pure can visit
they must fast a whole day and half
pine, plan for a year or two
before they visit you

we will enshrine you in marble
from European shores
inlaid lapis lazuli, outside
peacocks in the garden
fountains bursting colours
we will worship you
your visage, your body anointed
in red, yellow
your face smooth turmeric paste
our lives, our desires, our dreams
shall writhe at your feet

we will worship you
in return you must burn
first from the inside:
dry out the desire
that keeps you awake
dried-twig-like crush under your feet
those dreams that glisten
forgotten in your eyes
thoughts that anger
want to tear you apart

you must wash it out
wring yourself bone-dry
the hard bones you must crush
until they cannot support
and you will crawl
jelly-like amorphous moulding
the way we want you to

next your skin
it must burn
flake, curl into itself
beautiful eyes unseeing
hands crippled
breast waist fingers lips
conjoined mass

you must burn
the insides the outsides
the brain the mind the soul
the heart the earlobes
the swirls of your stomach
the legs and the in between
consuming fire
burnt, suffering, left with nothing
nothing

But now you are a Goddess
we will worship you.

The subaltern cannot speak

Let us wait and gather here for the stroke of the thirteenth bell on the fourteenth day when the walls will curve and crack and the gods will bend down from their homes on mountains and rivers for on such a day she will speak.

She will lift her throat, that beautiful throat and cry long and dark into the night, the night that is darkness so deep and dense that the cry will get buried, then like a wild animal escape out of the rot and earth it is buried under, and run it will, and fill the forests.

Upon hearing this cry, wordless yet full of meaning, it will remind us about that we cannot see, the things inside our hearts and minds, and we will be thrown back to a past where we roamed the earth both in innocence and terror, and as we see our pasts we will heal and we will weep and cry and our voices will join with hers.

She will lift her face then, that beautiful face, and hearing the voices join hers will wonder how has it come to be, that the world cries together for her but the cries will form words and sentences and laws, and our voices will drown hers, so the subaltern will learn to be quiet again and whisper, not yet not yet.

The awaited bells will toll, the gods will come and go.

For Plath, for Love

Don't
Let us then recite Plath's poetry
Let us wear white bikinis and smile
up at the sky, blue in our hearts as in the heavens
Let us sing mad girl love songs and in its rhymes
search thunderbirds, hold the bird close
dip into its heart, tasting its blood, yours, mine
Let us find these Hughes-like men who love
deeply, amorously, thick-honeyed words
that choke so well, filling us, filling us
with still, deep water, cleansing and drowning
who know how to twist deep into us, severing
every self-belief, every little hope we have
burning away the mind-body-soul chain
Don't
Let us write, write crazily into the night
and let our words howl in the still dawn
and let us then open the oven door
and lie ourselves in, breathing in purist like
a single strain of air, lying still then, lying still
while our children are in their beds, dreaming
                                        dreaming.

Shakti

One day you will see
- the Neelakurinji flower that blooms blue, once in twelve years
- the Aurora Borealis that flashes across cold still skies
- the Mariana Trench's secret life in its blackest depths
- metal glowing gold in the fire, carbon pressured into diamond
- the pyramid of Mount Kailash and the peak of the Himalayas

You will see it in my eyes; the past, the future, both in this present
You will see it on my mouth, you will see it on my face, glowing forehead
where the mountains and trees and sun and moon and stars are etched
and your very gaze will change. You will see. Me. One day. In this life
                          or many lives after
                          In me. Shakti.

Christmas day walk

A turn of the road, and there lies the forest. Rains from the night and days, wet leaves, post autumnal. My feet slip. Sneakers. There are families walking. With dogs. A cheery Merry Christmas. Can't a woman, an Indian woman, be alone? Can she not walk these wooded paths, summer and winter and spring, with no dog or man or anyone to give her company? A slight incongruence. The skies. The nests. Somewhere a bird tweets. They called a social media channel after birdsong. Then changed it to an obtuse letter. There will be a big dinner today in homes. Turkeys sitting proud, legs apart, waiting to be carved. Like you carve my heart out every day. Unintentionally or not. I don't say. I will never say it. Instead I will walk along the woods. A great hole. The black hole. In the silence of the woods my feet will echo. Somewhere an egret will fly. You too will eat turkey with your friends, smiling. I imagine the smile, I imagine more. This could be another day. It could be Boxing Day. New Year's. I will finish my solitary walk and go back to write the saddest poem. Red holly bushes. Spider silk. A dog's paws run through the wet sticky leaves, more surefooted than mine. Home is not far.

Unsaid, Unwritten

Unseeing, unthinking
piece words unrelated
flowers in a vase
on the kitchen table
lark, larkspur, lavender

When the night calls
answer
in words swallowed
in a past forgotten
eels, egalitarian, eccentric

then it is morning
slicing sun through clouds
unopened eyes, sleepy sex
harvest, hyacinth, harbour

a month is over
the thought still shattered
ravaged and unformed
the words meant
to disappear in bloodstream
vapid, victory, vilify

like Rodin's thinker
count words on fingers
the tongue struggling still
to form the unformed
the pen curling, curling

to write the unwritten

The Waiting

Of all the gifts you have given me
It is this silence
I will remember you by
Solid bark-like, roots deep in
immovable ocean rocks
eroding gently or not at all
Oizys, daughter of Nyx
stands sentinel, howls nights

Fool

A promise   A prophecy
Broken   Untrue
    More fool who waits
    Patiently in clemency

    Or more fool who leaves
    And forget sans mercy

Things in the fridge

There are things rotting in the fridge
the yoghurt we bought some days ago
our footsteps loud in the quiet superstore
angry our eyes, enraged our voices, as we seethed
about the news in the papers; the kisses
not shared for years coiling in that anger
you agreed with some, I disagreed with some
never the same things, and our footsteps grew angrier
as we argued louder, louder, the echoes lodging
in the yoghurt, now watery, large flecks of green mould
decorating its whiteness. It has gone off
as has this, this packet of bean sprouts, healthy food
bought the day the fires raged
humans howled and animals cried human tears
there's ash, broken bits of bones in the sprouts
and this meat, delicate-pink, we had bought the morning
they broke god's own house and danced on its ruins
as they have been doing for centuries
used drones over cities and maimed the children
the meat now mould-green, bright saffron, the smell drowns
the citrus deodorant in the fridge, and this Philadelphia
bought yesterday at news-time, as leaders spoke,
has sprouted large green spores on its soft cream cheese body
the leaders, from countries, where we live, where we love
where we were born, where we holiday, they talk louder
the acquiesced gather, the applause gets stronger
the narrative the same, the hate the same, and the voices all together
rise so high, so fast, and escape out of windows
over the houses and sweep, sweep across
those crimson skies, those drying rivers, those sinking mountains
and here in the fridge, more and more things rot.

Finding a Prayer

If this disheartens, the news heavy with statistics
of deaths, of the unwell, of inept governments getting it wrong
the delicate balance between people and wealth creation
and if this relieves; seeing a flash of a rainbow strung high up there
hearing a song of the bird you have never seen before
knowing the ozone layer itself is healing, while the cries of humans keep rising
think back then, sweeping history, what mankind has done, and been through
the wars, the disasters, the anger, the hatred, we have killed and maimed
explored and invented, served and sacrificed, we have sung, we have loved
we have sunk in gutters, swum across rivers, we have survived, we have lived
look back then and find the hope.

    Word a prayer
               hold it
                        call it your own.

A world like this

Is there such a world
where there's never been a drought
Is there such a sky
where the rains have never stopped
Is there such an earth
where the consciousness is one
Is there such a word
when spoken heals every wound
Is there such a touch
so deep, and is forever felt, never forgot?

More fool I, you may say
to ask a question, when the answer
is the same, whatever the language, wherever
in the world, more fool I, you may say

But what if, what if, such a moment does dawn
what if somewhere the skies and seas have met
would it be my dream, purple hallucinations
or just the irrelevant rambling of a poet, failed?

The city, a body

We lie in fragrant baths, candle-lit, aroma of a thousand roses, our skin glowing
Our toes sink into miles of sand on the beach
Our tongues explode with fiery chillies, lychee flesh, a shot of tequila sharp with lemon.

We find parts of ourselves, parts we did not know existed
before the lover arrived, and we sit transfixed on rotating hammocks as our bodies merge
We fly into realms unknown, new experiences in cities.

In cities with rivers, London, Paris, Stockholm
In cities with cliffs and shores, Belfast, San Francisco, Cape Town
In cities with skyscrapers and seas, New York, Mumbai, Hong Kong.

Often an alley, a street, unknown, unseen, a museum, a library, forgotten, a park, hidden
we explore, we are lost, we forget, we find something we don't know
we had never touched before, and we are transported. Another city,
                like a body, full of possibility.

Growing old

We cover ourselves with the gold and the silks
of yesteryear. The scars and wrinkles have grown

Consumed the silk smooth body that shone and sat
all heavy gold, in another's arms

We cover and cover what we don't like
with what we have spent our lives collecting

Tortoise crab shells, an armour
When it is time to go, unknown to us

The cover falls, soft flesh exposed
Wrinkled and marked,
                              a life laid bare

Infinity

Curled like an amniote
Head sunk in hands
Do not respond
Instead curl tighter
Tighter so that it is harder to unfurl
The pain is excruciating.
        Immovable.

A circle is the infinite
The beginning, the end of things
In this circle, of fingers, toes, legs, forehead
Nothing can enter
And nothing must
Sit, curled in, when the tears fall
Nothing matters
In the silence, infinite.

Death, unknown

yes, yes, I know we come alone go alone but when we come may it
be to the sounds of love and arms roped in an embrace and when
we go, and when we go may there be at least one person next to us,
the one who has loved us for an instant even, you know

> *no one should have to die alone*

but you did, and at that instant, what was happening outside? Were
there birds in flight, those tropical ones that disappear in a flash
of colour or did a half moon rise or did bats speak to each other in
sonic whispers or did a woman murmur in her lover's ears, not now,
not today?

> *you didn't have to die alone*

and what about the others who knew you, the husband, the friend,
the lover, lover turned friend, friend turned lover, where was he?
where was anyone? the mother the father the sisters who are meant
to love, the brothers who are meant to protect, the aunts, the uncles
where were they in their worlds not knowing, not knowing, you
were slipping away

> *cold and alone*

and so we think, we wonder asunder, how did it come to this
did you call the moment or did the moment call you
illicit whispers from worlds away cracking the earth into two?

The body is no more

1
From all those years ago
I still remember
fingers and hands, toes and legs
a flatness lying in my arms
eyes shut, cheeks cold

when breath leaves a baby
the body howls, shrivels
into nothingness for days
months years

when breath leaves a parent
life-giver, creator, taken away
body garlanded, shrouded
the body grows a bit older

2
What can I write about our bodies
supine in bath water, shapes, a shadow
perfumed, candle glow, soap-suds
softening skin?

This body has travelled
mountains, beaches, shores
been more than itself
carried tightly curled foetuses
passed on its blood memories

You trace it, the thinness of the waist
the thickening of the stomach
You turn it around, we meet
together we are heaven bound

I protest; heaven is not enough
to forget others – lives dreamed not lived
the ones we loved, the ones who left

When breath leaves the body
it stiffens, a heavy rigidity
the only deliverance, legs spread and bodies emerge
from the primal places we visit, we inhabit

3
Your fingers on my face
your hands on my neck
when breath stops for a moment
then flows like brooks babbling through
like blood in the veins and arteries
of the body

You whisper, the sense of the body
is only true when combined, conjoined
You whisper, when the body is no more
this breath we have shared is forever

This, in our blood

we laugh so hard that our mouths turn inwards and lose shape
then paint smiles on, upturned scars, watch poppy fields turn blue
we dream of faraway lands where the flowers are red and fragrant
with peacocks and poems and picture-books and forests verdant

the song humming inside remains one of sadness
of something beautiful, breaking in a flash
a lover leaving mid-kiss on a sunlit evening in Venice city of water
bleeding, oozing, weeping sores even years after

memories rush back to bite; in the waves that come and go
shoals of sprat leap, fall, then die on our feet
even as we watch, even as the water trickles from under our toes
we are voiceless, eyes morose, vacant in our many faces

the abyss inside, the one outside, a desolate seascape mirror
deep down, the sadness in us, in our blood, our skin, our bones
reaches the skies in a whirling column, boomerang-like pirouettes
back towards us, as we sob; we sob, fragments of ash and vapour.

PART 2
The Runaway Poem

Crab self-defence

you are the one with the claws
pincers poised
fast to trap, hurt
yet you are the one who runs away
when all I was doing was innocent play
sidestep, run, along the vast seas

I have seen that shell broken
broken flesh open
and adorning many a dinner plate
see that fear seeps through
see how you judge me

I will wait silently
watch you walk sideways
walk back to me
I will wait
on the seashore
watch you scuttle along the sands
I will hold off my touch.

Drown

You didn't say a thing.
You didn't do a thing.
Those curious eyes watched.
Not sure why,
not sure what they thought.

I drowned. I struggled.
Thrashing as the water rose
in waves and whirlpools
I sank, you watched
You who had said, water
fall in, feel it, let go!
I did,
And you let me down.

The moon, your friend, is glistening low
It doesn't let me see the shore
But somewhere a lighthouse glows
Surely it will carry me through to morning
When at last the daylight shows.

My Swan

In your pure whiteness I lie

The cold beak, webbed feet stroke my heart
I fall, shut my eyes in the darkness
to feel the depth, the newness
Where are you taking me?

in this journey of bruises and blood?
indifferent beak, beady eyes
haunt me, the wounds you give
bleed and burst, submerging senses

Stillness then in the depths
of this vast dark river
the lungs now full and heavy
with precious cold water

I open my mouth to speak
instead of words there
floats out a white feather
stained pink at the top
                    In these feathery arms I die

(Based on *Leda and the Swan*, W. B. Yeats)

The Sunrise

Here am I, with open arms
nourishing succour
this is how life seeps
how the water speaks
how lush forests grow

and there you are
burrowed under the earth
in an unending den
proud of the shining eyes
of the glass doll
you mate with ceaselessly
until it breaks

while outside I weave
colours wondrous
If only you could see
and seeing could understand
what it means, my intensity!

A dream in parts

And I dream trees
the kind you rest on
green soothing peace
the kind you climb on
sun and shade, shadows born
like the words of your song

I dream flowers
busy petal clusters scenting
the body, a bracelet of jasmine
a necklace of frangipani
ever living, my very heart
and ribs adorning

I dream skin
soft golden, you knowing
my skin, what lies within
my fingers feeling
the hollow at the base of your throat
calling it home, resting, resting

I dream duvets
bedside windows over city streets
shapes curled in, past-sunrise post-sunset
imprints in the down
our bodies, our selves
wrapped, growing memories

and then I dream lights
soft molten, clothing skin golden
shining bright, winking in our eyes
bared souls, warm bed-laden sighs
while outside the city shimmers
kisses on the waters.

A song in adversity

Was it something I said
that you turned away your head?
Sent you a song, sent you a poem
You kept it aside as if a tome
but some day when it is all over, will you meet me
                               just once by the river?
The home is silent, the heart more so
Man's voice, still, along with the city
Outside the birdsong, no longer a whisper
I think back about those days of dreams
when we talked, we laughed, we imagined
meeting, in forgotten cities, a kissing of eternity
In these days of isolation, still I seek that connection
So someday then when it is all over, will you meet me
                               just once by the river?

So you want to be a poet?

Prepare then to set your watch, to a different time, where the hands of the clock
are measured in a thought, a feeling, or a word, where things are as slow
or fast, like sentences, sometimes ambling over lazily, sometimes rushing, rushing

Prepare then to be there, yet not really there, every instant, as you meet and greet
people, fantasising instead of being alone, with your pen loving its paper
or fingers astride a laptop; eagerly wanting to bring alive, to birth a poem

Prepare then to be suddenly thrown away, by a tornado, at times even a tsunami
sucked straight out of a day, down, down into labyrinth of ideas and words
Prepare then to have a poem, which sits in your heart

Prepare to nurture it, and wait for it to catch flight, apart
So you want to be a poet? Prepare then to have everything
and sometimes nothing at all

Untamed River

You snake across my heart
like a river through a city
everyone knows rivers
need dams and bridges
and other things

Who allows water
to flow unrestrained?
Enamoured I swim
Then shining water, I'm submerged

Then I watch parts crumble
as the current gets stronger
and I watch pasts sink
as the riverbed gets deeper

The Reluctant Love

1. The Exorcist

Slowly, slowly, feel my fingers
stroking your forehead
wiping away the five folds moulded firm
Exorcising you
of her with the long hair
sleeping cloud shaking serpents
of her with the anklets
drawing blood pricking memories
of her with the rings, on toes you sucked
dry lips burning mouth
of her with the tattoos
seared into your skin flaming
of her with the dulcet voice
the tongue poisoning you
colouring your throat blue

Your mind closes, as I try
Love, they are burning you dry!
Healing you, I try
I am the exorcist, I try.

2. The Poet

I will write you a poem
It will twist
into you
like a corkscrew
into stoppered Cabernet Sauvignon

It will drill itself
into your heart
like an augur
boring hemispheres

It will sit on your eyelids
until they close
unseeing the day
It will sift into your ears
until they can't hear
wolves yodelling full moon blues

I will write you a poem
to grow in you
evergreen boughs
suffocating weeds

I will write you a poem
to submerge your words
like rains dissolving earth
to stifle your very voice
so you can't offer obeisance
to the ones you do; many a muse!

3. The Birthing

What if this is the only time we will ever meet
our paths crossing once over lifetimes
in a room like this, with windows in the right place
and doors set the way doors always are, in a corner
what if this is the only place we will ever chance to be together?

You want a breeze, you wish a balcony with creepers
jasmine, lemon, where we can breathe a little;
the walls close in, all day

> *there is smoke, unfurling from a cigarette*

Then fingers taming what can't be
fabric that slips off skin like memories
collecting thoughts and acts like keepsakes
Why do the good ones slip away, like silverfish
through fingers, pools of water?

Dark threads rise for days after
There is wine, cold on lips, on the body
more, more, I need more

there is silence, the words we didn't say

What is never to be:
Why not the flowers I asked for
Why not the pictures to keep forever
Why not the doodles on palms
Why not a desire to let it linger
Why not a plan to whisper together
the poems which were to be birthed
unconceived now, always

there are songs, playing on as if for someone else

What then if this is the only time we will ever meet?
If we'd thought this, if we'd known that was it: the walls,
lights glaring on the bed, this,
this the promised eternity
nothing more to look forward to
would we have looked for a clue
glanced a moment at those vast mirrors
to find an answer in our bodies, curled, prostrate?

there in this now, a birthing that shall never be

Trilogy of the Inevitable

Part 1: The Leaving

I have been telling myself
I must leave soon
I have been picking moments
from this pile of memories
first, the second, the third
the last, and I have been packing

I have been removing things
the things you'd loved
in the first picture
yesterday the feet, today the face
wiped away with a cold flannel

Then faceless, footless, I move silently
picking bits of the nights spent
tracing maps on bodies, writing futures on the skies
(did we not know they drift away, these clouds?)
collecting shards of the mornings
spent sucking oranges from our blue-green bowl

Those jagged pieces of the cold anger and hot fury
of the first, the second and the other fights
I drop those in as well, whimpering baby memories
luxurious that morning after, as if a dip in a lake
on a burning summer day, brutally beautiful

Thus, I pack; my red holdall is filling fast
tomorrow it will be the fingers turn to leave
slowly, the neck, the tongue, until one day
it will be the turn of the navel

I have been telling myself to leave

in pieces, in parts, in shadowy whispers
all these years, and you remain unseeing
maybe when my scent leaves those sheets forever
maybe when my breath leaves and there is air
maybe when your fingers fall on emptiness
maybe, only then you will know I was once there.

Part 2: The Cutting

Noughts and negations
spread like rash on skin
like algae on the pond
in the unused back garden
words you have said
written in clear black
I don't feel the same anymore. It's not you, it's me
I don't, I won't, I can't (love) you

I slit through them
dangling strips of flesh
cold sharpness of the knife
on creaminess of the skin
how beautifully it cuts!

                        criss-cross, criss-cross
                        like a child drawing on mum's
                        favourite cloth
                        the strokes go here, there
                        criss-cross, criss-cross

A sweet droplet forms, like a raindrop on the windowsill
brimming red it grows, bubble-red it forms
ribbons of blood, bold on the legs

I slice through them
cutting through moonlight
darkening the night
snubbing out stars that try to glimmer
submerging the whole earth in darkness for aeons ever

                    criss-cross, criss-cross
                    like a child drawing on mum's
                    favourite cloth
                    the marks filling the surface
                    criss-cross, criss-cross

A sweet bead of blackness forms, drops onto the body
pools, grows, forms lakes, rivers, seas of darkness
moulding the mind, drowning the soul, the weeping soul

I cut up then, this skin, like I shred paper in bits
I hammer, I scream
elevating pain, the cutting, mine, only mine.

Part 3: The Healing

See, it's autumn, then it's winter
and when everything dies, they heal
                            under the earth
these little daffodils bulbs I've planted
they grow don't they, every spring?
life within, life grows, it heals
so why not these wounds?
these ruptures will patch
skin, nerves, capillaries heal

                            everything changes
why not then this pain
that sits many splendoured
taking forms, shape-shifting
someday it will stop biting
stop stinging and start scabbing
time it heals they say; hardens
the skin over these wounds, then heals

                            so will I
become myself, like yesterday again

before there was a you, before you
ripped in so deep, ripped me so true
slowly, again, it will happen, I will heal.

You, soulmate

My love, who consoled me when I broke
held my fingers until they turned whole
while outside the moon and rivers sang a tune
even as the night caressed us into a mutual ruin

And that other love, the one who sang wild songs
clinging, fulfilling me whole in his praise of beauty
so young and changing, a life different from mine
no wonder then, he didn't stay very long

Then the quiet love who whispers about water as if he knows
moon tides and planets and stars and how everything works
Rain all night, the shy one with the dimples and smiles
Over, the chase, moments climax, like the others, he too goes

These stories I have for you, my love, my soulmate true!
An eternity away, searching, I ask, which one, which one was you?

Touched

Like the gold glint
On red autumn leaf
Like the moonlight
On gable rooftops
Like early morning mist on
Petals and gossamer
Like the deepest breath
At night time sleep
Like underground streams
That sing beneath deep earth
Like violets in the sun opening
Under wide expanses skies
Touched.
                    Touched!

Moon by night

Moon, you full moon tonight
just like that other night.
We stood together, watching you hang in the sky
chandelier, giant bauble, we stood there unaware
We stood in the middle of the road.
A car advanced, its lights on our forms.
I would have continued standing there watching you.
He noticed first, stepped away, towards me.
Tonight, you are the same, like that other night.
Cold moon, lucky moon, you dazzle.
My story is incomplete, doomed to remain so.
Carry my message, won't you?
Remind him of that night when you and I dazzled.
He'd noticed only one of us
 He still sees only one of us.

Love stories are sweet

I was busy, collecting stars for
you, pieces of the sun
A golden box to store everything
All along you were busy, scattering
our moments, words, silences
and wanting something new

Our heartbeat was
unstoppable
Yet you stopped, me
Dervish like we would have
loved, had you not stopped, me

They ask me, who heeds a song?
Words are not forever, they don't last long
But the voice that had called out to me
Was sometimes a command, sometimes a plea

Two broken pieces, either come together
Into a perfect whole, fitting each other
edges and curves, or crumble further
Jagged and hurting
I don't know
If we could have been creator
Broken selves together

Learning to unlove you
Is as hard as unlearning to get hurt by you
Forgetting loving you
If there is such a thing!
Finally gone the chill, why think of winter's silence
Or what is not here, a dry summer's sting?
My love, have you forgotten! It's your turn to sing
Write to me, this, this cherry-blossomy spring

Be that man

you know the one who will wake up wake me up with a bit of the
night skies, a slice of the moon glowing alive in his eyes
and in his arms hold slivers of yesterday and today and tomorrow
tied together in iridescent pieces and whisper about the caves we
have lived in the lives past
the skies we have conquered together and flown over oceans vast

the rivers we have swum in with dolphins and coloured fish brush-
ing against our limbs
the beaches we have walked sand trickling on toes while you've run
across and got a tender coconut
water drips from our mouths as we kiss

and be that man who holds me like a feather light slender gor-
geous, like I'm a stone heavy with love wonder and experience
and be that man who wants to love against the walls of the museum
Monet's lilies and Gauguin's women watching
or on the desk at home or on the grass near a cold gurgling stream

and that man who writes long and deep into the night of poetry of
war and peace and knows when to give and when to hold back

and be that man who knows that making love on the windowsill is
the best in afternoons full of drizzling rain in a tropical country
or on the fifteenth floor watching Christmas lights swarm London city

be that man who knows that the best love is had when one is angry
and wanting to rage and bite through the skin and the blackness
which is outside
and knows the way one feels just trapped, trapped in your limbs
and like in a box where despair is solid and growing like dark
smoke and all the cries in the world can't be heard

so be that man who knows how that feels how sound remains in

the throat sometimes stuck like a stone lodged in heavy clay
and when one speaks there is nothing no voice no whisper
and be that man who knows how to rub the small of my back then
speak sing and shout primal screams together to mark the day

my love, be that man, just be that man.

The Runaway Poem

Part 1

The poem I want to write for you
Will be about many things
Long fingers on guitar strings
Lotuses and Oms inscribed
Massages, hands stroking a bare back
as candles drip, and the day dwindles
into starlit evenings. Forest walks,
where the moss grows soft, a rustic bench.
The dog's leash held firm on a finger.

It will be about music and words
strung into poetry. Deep waters unknown,
shallow waters frothy.
At times a stream, dip in happy and gurgling
At times restlessness, the depth untested.
It will be about grass and butterflies
Bats even, about letting mice go
into freedom, as carefully as a bird
or even a soul.

It will be about whispers
and that bit of laughter
that often hangs
on to the tail of your words
About silent storms, tornado like,
then the rainbows. Joy like nothing other
and despair like none
The weight of silence and the lift of surprise.

Part 2

I try to write this poem about you
It runs off the page into the next
and on to the next.
It races out of the notebook.

I write again on embossed paper
with feather tip pens. Glorious, blue soft feathers.
I write in my best handwriting and my worst.
I call myself names, some lovely, some not
I try to write this poem, staying up all night.

Walk for days along the seaside, jellyfish blobs
on wet sand. Crabs dart sidewise into sparkling sand.

I walk in forests, where great trees grow and fall
I walk in dark cemeteries, where the wind speaks to me
lost, lost in the darkness, in ruin.

I walk on water, the waves seem to part
Sometimes I drown, breath disappearing
Other times I fly, as if with albatross wings.
Sometimes the poem slithers and hisses at me
angry that it is still not complete.

Often it is quiet, still,
as I heal, shape, decorate it.
Then sometimes it lies across me
takes me into my dreams and morphs, a lullaby
fingers stroking my face as I fall asleep.

Part 3

I did it then. I wrote a poem about you
It ran away at night. I wrote it again in the day

I kept it in a glass box, red rose petals
                        and bits of gold decorating the inside
Shimmering lid on to keep safe, words
                        patterned Chantilly lace

Still it ran away with a hop and a dart
flew with a push of wings I didn't know it had

Then in the sunset skies, I saw rainbows
        shooting stars, meteors, Aurora dancing
Then in my words, I saw the world
                  the entire world all crested, shining

Acknowledgements

Thank you Caro Clarke for the early edits and shaping the manuscript. Thank you Lynn Michell and the Linen Press team for loving the manuscript enough to make a book. To all the editors who have published my poems over the years, thank you for the encouragement.

Implications – Published in *May We Borrow your Country* (Linen Press, UK, 2018) and *Organisational Aesthetics* (2021) and Iamb Audio poetry Audio
The poet in business – Published in the journal Organisational Aesthetics (2021)
Not knowing, Migration – Published in journal The Lake UK (May 2018) and anthology May We Borrow your Country (Linen Press, UK, 2018)
Turmeric, Shakti, drown – Published in Setu magazine (November 2022)
Turmeric – Also published in Indian Yearbook of Poetry (Hawakal Publishers, 2023)
Unsaid, Unwritten, For Plath, for love – Published on Iamb audio poetry (2021)
Leaving – Published in Dragonfly Arts Magazine USA (2020)
Exorcist, Poet, Birthing – Published in Sarasvati 057, UK (August 2020)
Death Unknown, Healing – Published in The Bombay Review (April 2020)
A Dream in Parts – Published in Turnpike magazine (Sept 2019)
Sadness is a boomerang, Unsaid Unwritten, Three poems for my reluctant love – Published in Punch magazine (2019)
The Making of a Goddess – Published in New Asian Writing (April 2018)
The body is no more; For Plath, for love – Published in Usawa Literary Magazine (Dec 23)
Unbound Feet – Published in Tabula Rasa (Linen Press UK 2023)
The Swan; Death, Unknown; This, in our blood; Implications, Unbound Feet – Published in Converse, contemporary English Poetry anthology (Pippa Rann Media UK and Penguin India, 2022)
Be that man – Second prize in Momaya Press competition and published in anthology Love (Momaya Press, 2018)
Finding a prayer, A world like this – Published in anthology Hibiscus (Hawakal Publishers, May 2020)
You, soulmate – Published in the Roseate Sonnet anthology (Authors Press, 2020)
Unsaid, Unwritten; Three poems for my reluctant love; Be that man – Published in Lothlorien Poetry journal (February, 2024)
There are things in the fridge, Prayer, This, in our blood – Published in the anthology Don't Look Now (Linen Press, UK, 2025)

www.ingramcontent.com/pod-product-compliance
Lightning Source LLC
Chambersburg PA
CBHW042301030526
44119CB00066B/840